'Know the Game' series

RUGBY UNION FOOTBALL

Contents

FOREWORD

The Rugby Football Union supports and fully approves of all efforts which are made for the good of the game of Rugby Football. During the last few years much thought has been given to the basic principles of the game, to the skills, techniques and methods of coaching, and it is appreciated that the publishers of this booklet do all they can to keep it up to date and in keeping with modern ideas.

This latest edition of Rugby Union Football in "Know the Game" series should prove interesting and most helpful to beginners and less experienced players.

R. E. Prescott

Secretary, Rugby Football Union

ADMINISTRATION OF THE GAME

The Game of Rugby Football is controlled by the International Rugby Football Board—a body on which the four Home Unions and the Unions of Australia, New Zealand and the South African Rugby Football Board are represented.

The Home Unions, namely, the Rugby Football Union, the Scottish and Welsh Rugby Unions and the Irish Rugby Football Union together with the Unions of Australia, New Zealand and South Africa have two representatives each on the Board. The control of the game is therefore international in character.

Primarily, The International Rugby Football Board frames and interprets the Laws of the Game of Rugby Football. In addition it settles all questions concerning the Game which are international in character, it settles all questions connected with International Matches, or arising out of International Matches, and it controls all matters which are relative to the tours of teams representing the National Unions. Historically it is interesting to note that it meets annually on the morning of, or the day preceding, the England-Scotland International Match. Other meetings are held when necessary.

The Laws promulgated by the Board are binding on all matches played in the Home Countries and in the other countries represented on the board. Some variations of the Laws are permitted in domestic matches played in Australia and New Zealand. These two Unions are allowed to practise the variations which were in force at the time the Australian and New Zealand Unions joined the Board. In International Matches in those countries however no variations from the Laws are permitted.

Rugby Football is played throughout the British Commonwealth. In addition to the countries already mentioned Rugby Football is played in Canada, U.S.A., British Columbia, Ceylon, India, Kenya, Malaya, Pakistan and Trinidad; and there are Rugby Football Clubs in such places as Kuwait.

Membership of a National Union is restricted to the Clubs within that country. Eligibility for membership of the Rugby Football Union is open to all Clubs and Unions overseas, excepting the other Unions on the International Rugby Football board, within the British Commonwealth of Nations playing Rugby Football. Thus the Rugby Football Union represents on the Board not only the Clubs and Unions in England, but those abroad as well.

Each Club or Union sends a representative to the General Meetings of the appropriate National Union, at which, for instance changes in the Laws of the Game can be proposed though they do not become operative until ratified by the International Rugby Football Board.

The Federation Francaise de Rugby with its headquarters in Paris governs the Rugby Football Game played in France.

The Rugby Football Union is further sub-divided into constituent bodies, comprising the Royal Navy, Army, R.A.F., Counties or Groups of Counties, Oxford and Cambridge Universities and also the Central District (for those Clubs not allocated to any other Constituent Body).

Each Constituent Body provides a representative to the Rugby Football Union Committee whereby each Club is represented on that Committee.

The Constituent Bodies have delegated powers to act on the Rules as to professionalism and to hold enquiries and to inflict punishment in cases where a player is ordered off the field.

International Matches are arranged through the Board, games being arranged each season between the four Home Unions and the Federation Francaise. Teams from Australia, New Zealand and South Africa visiting Britain play representative teams of each of the four Home Unions and, on occasions, the Federation Francaise.

County Championship Matches or district matches are arranged by the respective Union, usually in the form of a Union " knock-out " competition on a territorial basis.

Club Matches are arranged by individual Clubs, but no Club may undertake a foreign tour without permission of its Union. Similarly no foreign Club may be invited to tour without that permission.

THE GAME

The game of Rugby football is played by two teams, each with fifteen players. The object of the game is to score tries and kick goals. A try is scored by a player grounding the ball in his opponents' in-goal and a goal is scored by kicking the ball between the opponents' goal posts above the cross-bar.

Scoring a goal

A try counts four points. A goal scored from a try counts six points when the try itself does not count.* A goal scored from a free kick or a penalty kick, or a dropped goal, counts three points.

The team with the highest number of points wins the match.

The diagram opposite shows the markings and dimensions of the playing area, which should be as near as practicable to the maximum dimensions.

*These new values are to operate for an experimental period up to and including 1972/73 season.

Scoring a try

THE FIELD OF PLAY

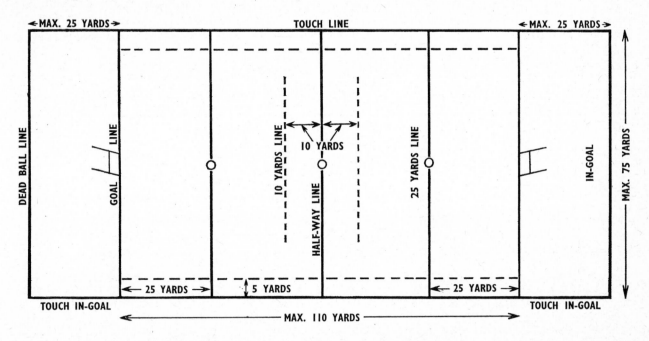

Marking lines should be clearly defined, uniform in width—not more than 4 inches wide and made with whiting or chalk. Ruts should not be cut in the turf.

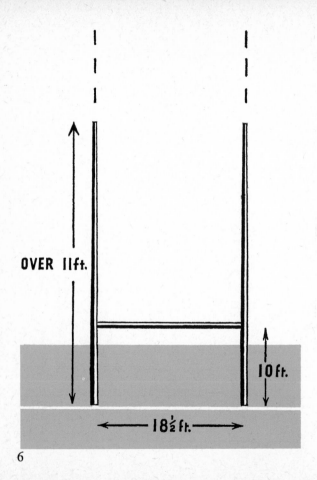

OVER 11ft.

10 ft.

18½ ft.

Goal Posts

The goal posts are two upright posts joined by a cross-bar, and are placed in the middle of the goal line. Dimensions as shown in the diagram.

For the purpose of judging a kick at goal, the upright posts are considered to extend indefinitely upwards and thus the taller the posts the easier the task of the adjudicating official.

The cross-bar must not extend beyond the goal posts.

Flag Posts

Flag Posts are placed at the corners of the goal line and the touch line, and to mark the 25 yards and halfway lines. The posts should be upright, but not too firmly fixed, so that they will give way should a player fall against them. They are usually about four feet high. Flag Posts may also mark the corners of the dead ball line and the touch-in-goal lines. In the case of those marking the halfway and 25 yard lines the flag posts are normally placed approximately one yard outside the touch line.

6

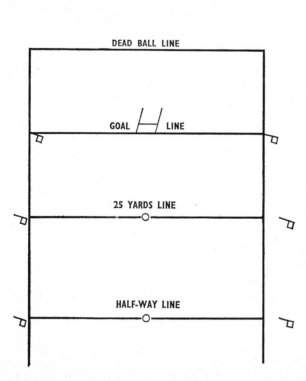

DEAD BALL LINE

GOAL ⌐ LINE

25 YARDS LINE

HALF-WAY LINE

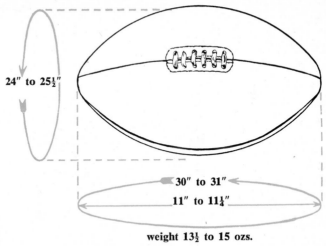

24″ to 25½″

30″ to 31″

11″ to 11¼″

weight 13½ to 15 ozs.

The Ball

The game is played with an oval ball, the outer casing of leather enclosing an air inflated bladder. The dimensions and weight are shown.

Nothing should be used in the construction which might injure the players. The lacing should be given careful attention in order that the outer casing is neatly closed.

7

THE PLAYERS

There are fifteen players on each side with no substitution except in recognised trial matches, international matches, and matches in which National Representative teams or teams of international status are playing with the approval of the Board. A player can only be replaced on the advice of a doctor, and the injured player must not resume playing in the match.

There are no hard and fast rules governing the names of the positions occupied by the players, and the numbers worn by them, but the usual custom adopted in Great Britain is illustrated in this diagram, which shows the line-up for a scrum.

Team consists of:

Forward Unit
- Front Row Forwards
- Second Row Forwards
- Back Row Forwards (loose forwards —Nos. 6, 7, 8)

Back Unit
- Half Backs
- Threequarter Backs
- Full Back

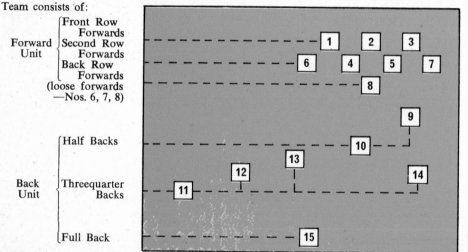

1. Prop Forward (*loose head*).
2. Hooker.
3. Prop Forward (*tight head*).
6. Flank Forward.
4.
5. } Lock Forwards.
7. Flank Forward.
8. No. 8 Forward.
9. Scrum Half Back.
10. Stand Off (or Fly) Half Back.
11. Left Wing Threequarter Back.
12. Left Centre Threequarter Back.
13. Right Centre Threequarter Back.
14. Right Wing Threequarter Back.
15. Full Back.

No. 9. the " Scrum half ", is the player who places the ball in the scrum.

No. 2. the " Hooker ", is the player who attempts to " rake " the ball from the scrum with his foot.

PLAYERS' EQUIPMENT

The players of one team all wear the same coloured shirts and shorts. They are usually numbered, each number indicating the position of the wearer.

Players should be smart in appearance. A smart team is not necessarily a good team, but a good team is invariably of smart appearance.

A player should take great care of his boots—clean them thoroughly and keep the leather in good condition. Long studs are more useful on soft grounds than short studs, but they must not be more than $\frac{3}{4}$ in. in length, and must be of leather, rubber, aluminium, or approved plastic. Studs should be securely fastened; the screw-in type are much safer than the nailed-in kind. The referee can order a player to remove any part of his equipment which is likely to cause injury to other players, e.g., projecting nails on boots, rings on fingers, buckles, leather shoulder pads, etc.

OFFICIALS

In all matches a referee and two touch judges must be appointed or agreed upon by the two captains.

The Referee

Is responsible for imposing penalties for infringement of the laws of the game during play; he is the sole time-keeper and judge; and he keeps the score. To do this he carries a whistle (and a spare) which he blows when he wishes to stop the play, a notebook and pencils. He should also have a coin with which the opposing captains can toss for choice of ends; and also a watch.

His dress should be of a colour easily distinguishable from the colours of the players' shirts.

The referee must allow extra time for delays and may also stop a match if he thinks that full time cannot be played. For repeated infringement of the Laws, he must report a player to the Constituent Body having jurisdiction over the Club to which the player belongs, and he must dismiss from the playing area any player who has already been cautioned for Obstruction, Foul Play, or Misconduct. Any player ordered off the field must be reported by the referee to the organisation under the jurisdiction of which the game is being played.

Having given a decision, the referee cannot alter it except if he gave the decision without knowing that a touch judge's flag remained raised. In certain cases, should the referee stop the game for an infringement, the non-offending team may as a result lose the advantage they may have gained and perhaps the opportunity to score: in such a case the referee should allow play to continue and the non-offending team to maintain its advantage.

The success of the game depends largely on the referee, who should keep up with the play, be neutral yet consistent at all times in his decisions, and limit stoppages to a minimum.

Goal

Found Touch

The Touch Judge

Holds up his flag to show when and where the ball, or the player carrying it, went into touch, or touch-in-goal, and he indicates from which point and also by which team the ball should be brought back into play. He lowers his flag when the ball has been thrown in properly. If the ball is thrown in by a player of the team not entitled to do so, or if the player throwing in the ball puts either foot into the field of play, he keeps his flag raised, and unless the opposing team has gained an advantage the ball must be thrown in again correctly. He assists the referee to judge on kicks at goal by standing behind a goal post of the defending team and signals, by raising his flag, that the ball has gone over the crossbar.

DURATION OF PLAY

In International matches the game lasts for two periods of 40 minutes each.

In other matches, the duration of the game is agreed upon by the respective teams.

Play is divided into two halves separated by an interval of not more than five minutes. At half-time the teams change ends.

The referee blows his whistle to indicate half-time and " no side ". He should not blow for half-time or " no side " until the ball is dead. If a try has been scored, or a free kick or penalty kick has been awarded, the referee must allow play to continue until the ball becomes dead again before blowing for half-time or " no side ".

Choice of Ends

Before the game starts the home captain tosses a coin giving the visiting captain the call. The winner of the toss may choose:

(*a*)   To kick off.

              or

(*b*)   Which goal-line his team will defend.

If he chooses (*b*) his opponents take the kick off.
After the interval the kick off is taken by the team which did not kick off to start the game.

LAWS OF PLAY

Advantage

Except that the ball must be kicked off according to Law 10, and must not come out of the scrum except as laid down in Law 20 (10), the advantage Law applies to every other Law.

The Kick Off

After the choice of ends the teams line up in their respective halves of the field and the game is commenced by a place kick taken by any player of the team awarded the kick off. The ball is placed at the centre of the half way line and must be kicked forward beyond the opponents' 10 yards line. All players of the kicker's team must remain behind the half way line until after the ball has been kicked forward. The game is recommenced in a similar manner after a goal has been scored and at the start of the second half of the game.

When the ball is kicked off it must reach the opponents' 10 yards line, unless an opponent first plays it. If not, it is either kicked off again, or a scrum is formed at the centre, at the opponents' discretion. The opposing team must not stand within the 10 yards line and must not advance over that line until the ball has been kicked, otherwise the kick off is taken again.

The ball may be kicked into touch from the kick off provided that it travels at least 10 yards forward and pitches in the field of play. If the ball pitches into touch beyond the 10 yards line, touch-in-goal, or over the dead ball line, the opposing team has the choice of a scrum at the centre, another kick off, or may accept the kick. If they accept the kick, the ensuing line-out shall be formed at the half-way line, or where the ball crosses the touch line if that place is nearer to the kicker's goal-line.

After the kick off the ball may be kicked or picked up by any player who is on-side.

13

Ball In and Out Of Play

The ball is out of play when it goes into touch, when it is made "dead", or when the referee stops the game.

Touch

The ball is in touch when:

(*a*) It touches the ground on or over the touch line (the touch line itself being out of play).

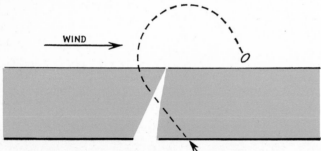

WIND →

(*b*) It crosses a touch line (in the air) and is then blown back, unless it is then caught immediately by a player in the field of play.

(*c*) A player carrying it steps on, or touches the touch line, or the ground outside the touch line.

The ball is not in touch when a player standing in touch kicks a ball which has not crossed the touch line.

NOTE:—A player is not allowed to throw the ball deliberately into touch, and should he do so a penalty is awarded against him. See page 11.

Throw in

When a ball goes into touch in the normal course of play, or is carried over the touch line by a player, a throw in is awarded to the non-offending team.

When the ball is in touch, the place at which it must be thrown in is as follows:—

  (i) when the ball goes into touch from a penalty kick, or from a kick within twenty-five yards of the kicker's goal line; at the place where the ball went into touch.

 (ii) when the ball pitches directly into touch after being kicked otherwise than as stated in (i); opposite the place from which the ball was kicked or at the place where it pitches into touch if that place be nearer to the kicker's goal line.

(iii) on all other occasions when the ball is in touch; at the place where the ball went into touch.

It is thrown straight into the field of play so that it is first played at right angles to the touch line and must travel at least five yards before it touches the ground or a player. The player throwing the ball in from touch must not put either foot in the field of play. When the ball is thrown in incorrectly, the other team may either throw in the ball or have a scrum fifteen yards from the touch line.

Until the ball has touched a player or the ground 5 yards from the touch line, the players participating in the throw in must not, with either foot, go beyond an

imaginary line at right angles to the touch line through the spot where the ball went into touch.

Pushing, charging or in any way interfering with another player in the line out is prohibited unless the other player has the ball in his possession, when he may be lawfully tackled. Penalty for these infringements is a Penalty Kick fifteen yards in from the touch line.

The team throwing in the ball controls the length of line out.

Touch-in-Goal

The ball is in touch-in-goal:

(*a*) When, not being in the possession of a player, it touches a corner post, or touches or crosses a Touch-in-goal line.

(*b*) When the ball in a player's possession, or a player carrying it touches a corner post or touches a Touch-in-goal line or the ground beyond it.

The flag shall not be regarded as part of the corner post.

Play is restarted by a drop-out taken by the defending team, from within the 25 yard line.

Dead Ball

If the ball crosses a goal-line after last touching an attacking player and is subsequently kicked or carried over the dead ball line by a defender, the game is restarted by the defending team taking a drop-out from within the 25 yards line.

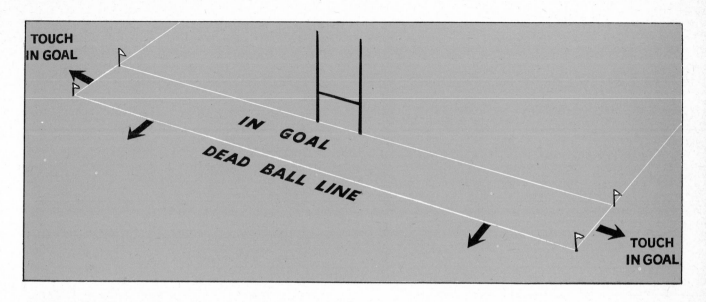

TOUCH IN GOAL

IN GOAL

DEAD BALL LINE

TOUCH IN GOAL

The ball is dead when an attacking player kicks or carries the ball over his opponents' goal-line and it subsequently crosses the touch-in-goal lines or the dead ball line; or if an attacking player infringes in his opponents' in goal. The game is restarted by the defending team drop kicking from within the 25 yards line. A player who throws the ball deliberately from the field of play into touch-in-goal or over his own dead ball line will be penalised; but a player may do so from his own in-goal provided the throw is not forward.

GROUNDING THE BALL

If a defending player first grounds the ball in his own in-goal after the ball is kicked over by an attacking player, a touch down is awarded. The game is restarted by the defending team drop-kicking on or behind the 25 yards line.

The ball must reach the 25 yards line and all the kicker's team must be behind the ball when he kicks it. The opponents must not charge over the 25 yards line.

If a defending player touches down after the ball has been heeled, kicked, passed, knocked or carried over his own goal-line by one of his own team, a scrum is formed 5 yards from the goal-line opposite where it was kicked, passed or carried over, and the attacking team puts in the ball.

In the diagram on the right the ball has been touched down by the defending team, but the scrum is taken 5 yards from the goal line opposite the place where it was kicked back.

To ground the ball a player must place his hand or hands or arm or arms on it, whilst it is on the ground, in such a way that he exerts a downward pressure on the ball. To touch the ball may not be to ground it.

He may also ground it if falling on the ball as long as it is anywhere under the front of his body from waist to neck inclusive.

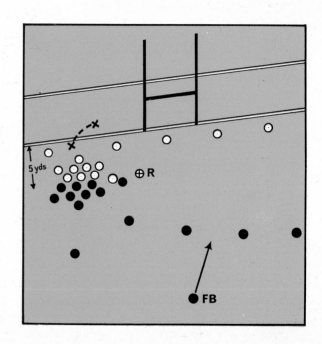

THE TRY

A try is scored by an attacking player first grounding the ball in his opponents' in-goal.

An on-side player can score a try by grounding the ball in his opponents' in-goal after it has been kicked over the goal-line by one of his own team, or has been passed, knocked, or kicked over the goal-line by an opponent.

If, in a scrum, one team push the other team over the latter's goal line, the attacking team can score a try by grounding the ball. (Similarly, if the defending team ground the ball, the referee will award a touch down.)

If an attacking player carrying the ball touches the referee in his opponents' in-goal a try is awarded at that place.

The referee should award a try to a player if, in his opinion, the player would have probably scored but for unfair play or unlawful interference by the defending team. In this case the try is awarded between the posts.

The goal-line is itself within the in-goal area, so that a player may score by grounding the ball on the goal-line.

THE GOAL

A goal may be scored by:

(*a*)   Converting a try.   (*c*)   A penalty kick.

(*b*)   A drop kick during play.   (*d*)   A free kick.

A goal cannot be scored from a kick off, drop out, or a punt.

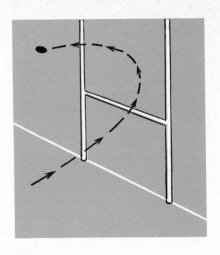

A goal is allowed if:

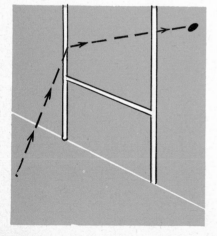

(*a*)   the ball passes over the cross-bar and is then blown back by the wind.

(*b*)   the ball hits the cross-bar or goal posts and re-bounds over the cross-bar.

It is not a goal if the ball first bounces on the ground before passing over the cross-bar.

Converting a Try

A team scoring a try is awarded a kick at goal, to attempt to " convert " the try into a goal. Thus a converted try scores five points.

The kick at goal is taken from any point within the field of play opposite the spot where the try was awarded, as shown in the diagram.

The kick may be a "place kick" (that is, the ball is kicked from the ground, and it may be placed in position by the kicker) or a drop kick.

The kicker may choose to have a player hold the ball for him (e.g. in a high wind).

Players of the attacking team must remain behind the ball when the kick is taken.

Players of the defending team must stand behind their own goal-line until the kicker begins his run or offers

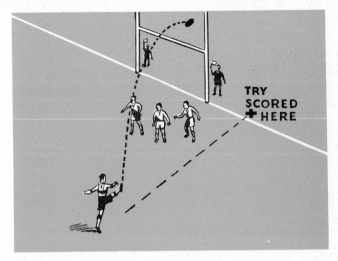

The place for a kick must be on a line, parallel to the touch line from where the try was scored.

to kick. They may then charge or jump, in an attempt to touch the ball.

If the kick at goal is unsuccessful the defending team restart the game with a drop kick from or behind the centre of the halfway line.

21

Goal from Drop Kick

An attacker during play may drop the ball and kick it directly on the rebound, i.e., the half-volley, over the cross-bar.

Goal from Penalty Kick

When a penalty kick is awarded the non-offending team may elect to attempt a kick at goal. The kick is taken from a point at, or behind, the place where the offence occurred, on a line through that place parallel to the touch line. The Kick may be a place kick or a drop kick and the kicker may place the ball.

All players of the offending team must retire without delay to a line parallel to the goal line and 10 yards from the spot where the offence occurred, or to their own goal line if that is nearer. They must remain motionless there, with their hands by their sides, until the ball has been kicked. Players of the non-offending team remain behind the ball while the kick is taken.

HANDLING

The ball may be passed, thrown or knocked from one player to another in any direction except forward.

Forward Pass

If a player throws the ball in a forward direction to one of his own team, the referee awards a scrum at the place where the infringement occurred.

If a player makes a forward throw but before he, or one of his team, touches the ball again an opponent gains possession, the game may be allowed to continue.

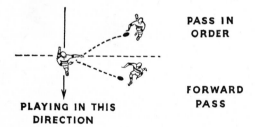

PASS IN ORDER

FORWARD PASS

PLAYING IN THIS DIRECTION

If the throw is not forward and the ball falls to the ground and then bounces forward, it is not an infringement and play continues.

Knock-On

A knock-on occurs when a player propels the ball with his hand or arm in the direction of his opponents' dead-ball line or when the ball, after striking the hand or arm of a player travels in that direction and touches the ground or another player.

If a player misfields the ball, it does not constitute a knock-on unless it travels directly from his hand or arm in the direction of his opponent's dead ball line. Should the ball fall vertically to the ground, it is not a knock-on. A player attempting to catch a ball (otherwise than direct from a kick) and not making a clean catch will not be judged to have knocked on even if the ball travels forward, provided that he gains control of the ball without making a second catch.

If a player attempting to pick up a ball propels it forward, whatever the distance, it is a knock-on.

A knock-on also occurs when a player in a line out, jumping for the ball, knocks it forward and then catches it cleanly.

After a knock-on or throw forward the ball is brought back to the place of infringement and a scrum is formed there unless the opposing team gains an advantage.

Not a Knock-on

Knock-on

If the ball is unintentionally knocked-on by a player who is in the act of catching it from a pass or direct from a kick, and is recovered by that player before it has touched either the ground or another player, it is *not* a knock-on.

If, in charging down a kick, the ball travels forward from a player's hands or arms, the referee does not stop the game for a knock-on unless he is actually attempting to catch it, and it goes to ground. A fair catch can be made from a knock-on.

Rebound

If the ball strikes any part of a player, other than his hand or arm, and then travels in the direction of his opponents' dead ball line, it is said to have "rebounded" Play continues, without interruption.

If the ball strikes a player's leg (from the knee to the toe inclusive), the player is deemed to have kicked the ball.

Should the ball touch a player's hand or arm and then strike another part of his body before travelling forward, it is a rebound and not a knock-on.

Knock-on

Rebound

THE SCRUM: THE RUCK

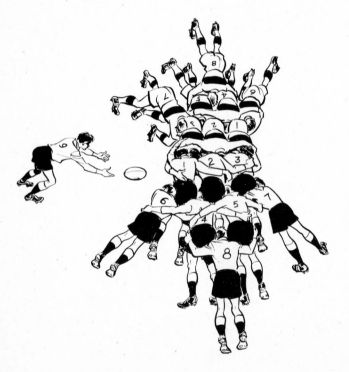

A **scrum** is formed by players of each team closing up in readiness to allow the ball to be put on the ground between them.

The scrum is ordered to restart the game after certain infringements. In most cases the scrum is formed where the infringement occurred. For infringements by a defending team in in-goal, the scrum is formed five yards from the goal-line. A scrum can only be formed in the field of play.

A **ruck** is formed by one or more players from each team in physical contact and on their feet closing round the ball when it is on the ground between them.

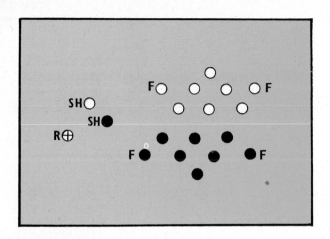

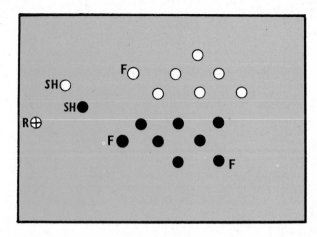

The Scrum

Any number of players may take part in a scrum, but three players shall form either front row of the scrum before the ball is put in. It is general practice for the scrum to be formed by the forwards of the two opposing teams.

The players of each front row shall bind firmly together while the ball is being put in and while it is in the scrum. All other players in a scrum must bind with at least one arm and hand around the body of another player of the same team.

There are two scrum formations adopted by different teams:

The 3—2—3 and 3—4—1 formations.

The advantages claimed for the 3—4—1 formation (left hand diagram) are that the flanking forwards (marked F) can break quickly from the scrum when the ball is heeled so that it is channelled from the scrum with greater control and a more effective concerted snap shove is possible. The 3—4—1 formation is generally favoured with variations such as 3—3—2, 3—3—1, etc., (right hand diagram), for forward link penetration with half-backs.

Putting in the Ball

The player putting in the ball (usually the scrum half) must:

(*a*) Stand one yard from the scrum midway between the two front rows.

(*b*) Put the ball in with both hands in a single movement from a level midway between his knee and his ankle.

(*c*) Pitch the ball on the ground immediately beyond the nearest first player.

The ball must also be put in straight along the middle line quickly.

The " middle line " is an imaginary line on the ground directly beneath the line formed by the junction of the shoulders of the players forming the respective front rows.

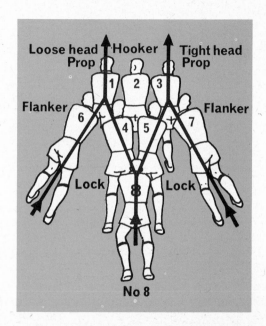

Ball Fairly in

The ball is not fairly in the scrum if it comes out at either end of the tunnel.

It can follow any other path to come out of the scrum. If the ball comes out of the scrum at either end of the tunnel the referee will order it to be put in again or he may award a penalty for wilfully kicking out.

28

Until the ball has touched the ground no player in either front row may raise either foot from the ground or advance it beyond the line of feet of his front row. The feet of the nearest players must be far enough back to leave the tunnel clear.

When the ball has left the scrum half's hands and is fairly in the scrum, it may be played as shown in the diagram at right.

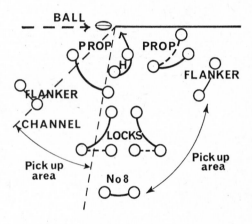

Principles of 3—4—1

1. Foot placings are as important as snap shove to provide correct channel to pick-up area.

2. Concentration should be on snap shove and lock.

3. Watch the mechanics—not 3—2—3 with flankers up.

4. Flankers pack down early at wide angle and stay there.

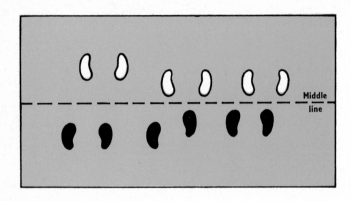

Middle line

While the ball is in the scrum a player must *not*, in order to get the ball

swing both feet; or

raise both feet off the ground at the same time; or advance both feet beyond the middle line of the tunnel; or

lower or twist his body so as to get nearer the ball, or in any manner liable to cause the scrum to collapse.

Scrum and Ruck Infringements

In either scrums or rucks: —

(*a*)   A player must not return the ball into the scrum or ruck by hand or by foot after it has come out.

(*b*)   A player lying on the ground must not interfere with the ball in any way and must do his best to roll away from the ball.

(*c*)   A player must not handle the ball, pick it up by hands or legs, or intentionally fall or kneel on it, unless the scrum or ruck has moved into either in-goal (see page 19).

(*d*)   A player must not do anything to cause the scrum or ruck to collapse.

(*e*)   A player must not add himself to the front row to make more than 3 players in that row.

TACKLING

A player holding the ball may be grasped round the body or legs by one or more opponents. If, as a result, the ball, still in the player's possession, touches the ground and the player is still held by the opponent, he is deemed to have been tackled. Or if the player is so held that there comes a moment when he cannot pass or play the ball, a tackle has occurred.

A tackle does not occur if a player is knocked or thrown **over by an opponent, even though the ball may touch the** ground. He may, therefore, pass the ball or get up and continue his run.

If the momentum of a player who has been tackled carries him with the ball into his opponents' in-goal and he grounds the ball there, the referee should award a try. For example, a player running at full speed and tackled from behind may slide along the ground with the ball in his hands for some distance.

If in such a case a tackled player crosses his opponents' goal-line before coming to a stop a try should be awarded.

After a Tackle

A tackled player, whether he has or has not been brought to the ground, must immediately release the ball, i.e., allow it to fall to or remain on the ground.

No player can pick it up before a tackled player lying on the ground has released it.

A tackled player, if lying on the ground, must release the ball at once, move his body away from it, and get up on his feet before playing it. Indeed, anyone on the ground after a tackle must get up before playing the ball.

Handing Off

A player may elude a tackle by " handing off " his opponent. This means he may push him off with the open palm of his hand. He must not strike or punch.

KICKING

There are three types of kick in the game: the Punt, the Drop Kick and the Place Kick.

The Punt

A player is said to punt the ball when he drops it from his hands and kicks it before it touches the ground. A punt is useful for finding touch or gaining ground but may not be used outside own 25 kicking direct into touch.

If the ball is kicked directly into touch from a point outside his own 25 yards area, either by a punt or drop kick, or from a mark (fair catch), a line out is given parallel to the point from which the ball was kicked.

The ball is kicked with the instep and an expert can impart a special motion to the ball which gives the kick extra length and accuracy.

A goal *cannot* be scored from a punt.

The Punt

The Drop Kick

A player drop kicks the ball when he drops it from his hands to the ground and kicks it immediately it rebounds.

A drop kick is used:

(*a*) To recommence the game from or behind the centre of the halfway line, after an unconverted try has been scored by the opponents (see page 21).

(*b*) To recommence the game from or behind the 25-yard line after a touch-down, or after the ball has gone into touch-in-goal, or over the dead ball line.

(*c*) To score a goal during play (see page 20).

The Drop Kick

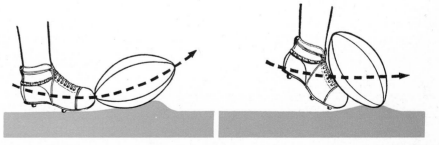

The Place Kick

The Place Kick

A place kick is made by kicking the ball after it has been placed on the ground for the purpose.

It is used:

(a)   To start the game and recommence it after the interval or after a goal has been kicked (see page 13).

(b)   To kick at goal after a try has been scored, in which case the kick is taken from any spot opposite where the try was scored and parallel to the touch line.

(c)   To kick at goal after the award of a penalty kick, the kick being taken from the spot where the penalty was awarded, or behind that spot on a line through it, parallel to the touch line (see page 38).

There are various ways of place kicking favoured by players, the two most popular being illustrated.

A good kicker takes infinite care at a place kick and, after sighting the goal, does not take his eye off the ball until after he has kicked it.

FAIR CATCH

A "fair catch" is made by a player who simultaneously:

(*a*) Catches the ball cleanly after it has been kicked, knocked or thrown forward by one of his opponents;

(*b*) Is stationary with both feet on the ground; and

(*c*) exclaims "Mark".

After a "fair catch" a free kick is awarded and this must be taken by the player making the "fair catch".

A player may not kick directly into touch unless kicked from own 25 area.

THE FREE KICK

The ball is kicked from the mark or any point behind it and the same distance from the touch line as the mark.

It may be a place kick, drop kick, or punt. If a place kick is taken the ball must not be handled by the kicker after it has been placed on the ground for the kick.

All players of the kicker's team must be behind the ball when it is kicked.

Players of the defending team may approach a line through the mark and parallel to the goal line and may charge:

(a) In the case of a place kick, as soon as the ball has been placed on the ground;

(b) In the case of a drop kick or punt, as soon as the kicker begins his run or offers to kick.

The ball must be kicked past the mark made, unless first played by an opponent, and if it does not reach the mark the referee orders a scrum at the mark.

For any infringement by the kicker's team the referee orders a scrum at the mark.

For any infringement by the defending team the referee disallows the charge, and if the kick has been taken, the kicker is allowed the option of another kick under the original conditions but without the charge.

THE PENALTY KICK

The referee awards a Penalty kick to the non-offending team in the case of certain infringements which can be grouped under the following headings:

(*a*)   Offside Play (see page 40).

(*b*)   Deliberate disobeyance of the laws.

(*c*)   Foul Play (see page 47).

(*d*)   Obstruction (see page 45).

The Penalty kick may be a drop kick, place kick, tap, or punt and is taken at or any point behind the spot where the infringement occurred but not nearer the opponents goal-line than 5 yards parallel to the touch line. The object of the kick may be either:

(*a*)   To score a goal from a drop kick or place kick.

(*b*)   To gain ground by kicking for touch.

(*c*)   To gain ground by kicking forward for the kicker's team to follow up and attempt to gain possession.

The tap penalty must be taken from the place where the offence took place. The ball may be played in any direction by the foot and then picked up. The penalised team must make every effort to retire without delay 10 yards from where the kick is being taken.

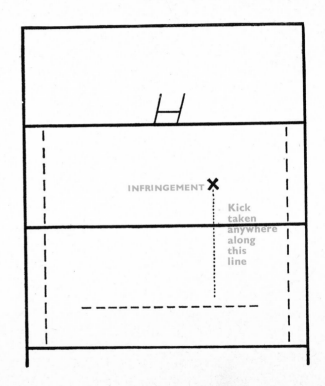

38

INFRINGEMENT

10 yds

When the Penalty Kick is taken, the following rules must be observed:

(a) All players of the kicker's team other than the placer for a place kick must be behind the ball when it is kicked. If one is in an offside-position, a scrum is formed at the spot where the kick was taken.

(b) Players of the defending team must retire without delay to, or behind, a line parallel to the goal-lines and 10 yards from the mark, or to their own goal-line, whichever is nearer.

(c) Players of the defending team must stand motionless with their hands by their sides until the ball has been kicked.

The kick or tap may be taken in any direction.

For an infringement by the opposing team the kicker is given another kick 10 yards in front of the mark or on the goal line, whichever is the nearer on a line through the mark parallel to the touch line.

NOTE:—A scrum may be taken at the mark by the non-offending team instead of a penalty kick.

OFFSIDE

A player is in an offside position when he is in front of a player of his own team who is in possession of the ball, or who last kicked or touched the ball. In such a position he must not play the ball, or approach or wilfully remain within 10 yards of an opponent waiting for the ball.

If a player in an offside position plays or attempts to play the ball, or tackles or attempts to tackle an opponent, or remains within 10 yards of an opponent waiting to receive the ball, the referee will award a penalty kick to the opponents at the place where the infringement occurred, or a scrum at the place

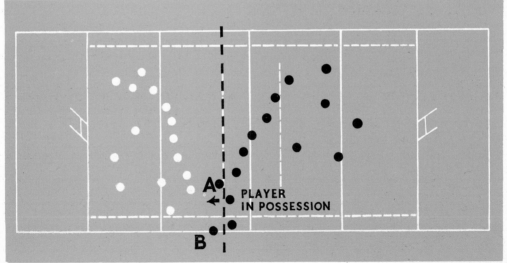

A and B are Offside

OFFSIDE PLAYER
INTERFERING WITH
PLAY

TACKLING FROM
OFFSIDE POSITION

where the ball was last played before the infringement occurred. The non-offending team has the option of either award.

The exceptions to the rule are offside play following a kick off, free kick, drop out or penalty kick, when a scrum is formed where the kick was awarded if one of the kicker's side gets in front of the kicker, except after a penalty kick, when the scrum is ordered at the place where the kick was taken.

The advantage law however applies in the case of a free-kick, drop-out and penalty kick.

Another exception occurs if the ball, or a player carrying it, touches a player who is accidentally offside, when a scrum is ordered at the place where the offside occurred.

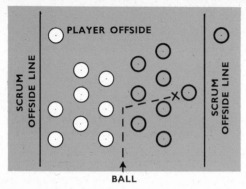

A player is also offside if:

(a) He enters the scrum from his opponents' side.

(b) While the ball is in the scrum he, not being in the scrum, nor either of the scrum-halves, fails to retire behind 'the scrum off-side line' (See diagram).

(c) When participating in the line out, before the ball has touched a player or the ground, he advances either foot in advance of the line of the throw, except in an attempt to catch the ball; or after the ball has touched a player or the ground, he, not being in possession of the ball, advances either foot in advance of the ball, unless he is lawfully tackling, or attempting to tackle, an opponent on the line. If he is not participating in the line out he must stand at least 10 yards behind the line of touch.

The penalty in all these cases is a penalty kick awarded to the non-offending team at the place of infringement, subject to the advantage law.

ONSIDE

A player in an offside position can be placed on-side, provided he is not within 10 yards of an opponent who has possession of the ball, by any of the following movements:

1. An " offside " player becomes " onside " when an opponent in possession of the ball has run 5 yards.

A kicks the ball forward, placing B in an offside position. X catches the ball, and when he has run 5 yards, B becomes onside and may tackle him.

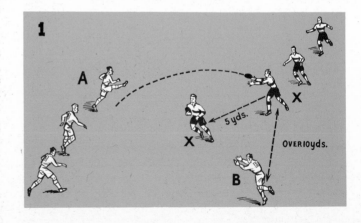

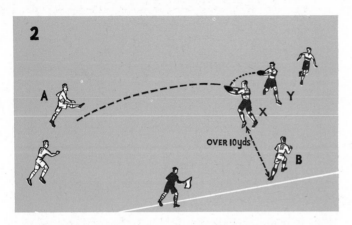

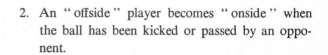

2. An "offside" player becomes "onside" when the ball has been kicked or passed by an opponent.

B is offside when A kicks the ball. The ball is caught by X who passes it to Y. B, who is NOT within 10 yards of X, is put onside by the pass by X to Y.

3. An "offside" player including the player who is within 10 yards of an opponent who is waiting for the ball, becomes "onside" when a player of his own team in possession of the ball has run in front of him.

When A receives the ball B and C are offside, but as A runs forward with the ball in his possession he passes B and C, placing them onside.

4. An " offside " player becomes " onside " when a player of his own team kicks the ball when behind him and then runs in front of him. Only the kicker can put the player onside, and he must be in the field of play or in in-goal, though he can follow up in touch or in touch-in-goal and return to the field of play or into in-goal to put the player onside.

A kicks the ball forward and B standing onside follows up quickly. B cannot put C onside by running past him—only the kicker can do this. Once B has touched the ball, however, all his own players behind him will be onside.

5. An "offside" player becomes "onside" when an opponent has intentionally touched the ball, provided that the opponent does not catch or gather it.

6. An "offside" player can place himself onside, by running back behind the player of his own team who last kicked the ball when behind him.

BALL TOUCHING REFEREE

If the ball, or a player carrying it, touches the referee in the field of play, a scrum is taken at that spot, unless the referee considers that neither team has gained an advantage in which case he shall allow play to proceed. If the ball in a player's possession, or a player carrying it, touches the referee in:

(a) That player's in-goal, a touch-down is awarded at that spot.

(b) An opponents' in-goal, a try is awarded at that spot.

If the ball, while in play in in-goal at either end and not held by a player, touches the referee or a touch judge:

(a) A touch-down will be awarded, if a touch-down would otherwise have been obtained, or the ball would have gone dead.

(b) A try will be awarded if a try would otherwise have been obtained.

If the ball, or a player carrying it, touches a spectator in in-goal the award made by the referee will be governed by the above laws. Should the issue be in doubt, the referee will decide in favour of the visiting team—it is the responsibility of the home team to keep spectators off the field of play.

OBSTRUCTION

Obstruction occurs when:

(a) A player holds an opponent not carrying the ball.

(b) A player charges, pushes or holds an opponent at the line out before the ball has touched a player or the ground.

(c) A player, not running for the ball, charges or obstructs an opponent not holding the ball.

(d) A player overtaking an opponent also running for the ball pushes him from behind.

(e) A player running for the ball charges an opponent also running for the ball except when it is a shoulder to shoulder charge.

(f) A player not running for the ball wilfully charges or obstructs an opponent who has just kicked the ball.

(g) A player with the ball in his possession after it has come out from a scrum, ruck, or line out attempts to force his way through his own forwards.

For any of these offences, a penalty kick is awarded at the place of infringement, or, in the incident shown in the sketch, either at the place of infringement or where the ball alights, at the option of the non-offending team.

Other cases of obstruction, not specifically covered by the laws, do occur in Rugby Football. Such cases are:

(a) A player carrying the ball intentionally, in the opinion of the Referee, runs into an offside player of his own team.

(b) An offside player "shielding" from an opponent a member of his own team who is carrying the ball, (see illustration), or a player who is not running for the ball preventing an opponent from so doing.

(c) An outside player in the scrum moving outwards and thereby preventing an opponent from getting round the scrum, even though he maintains contact with the scrum.

FOUL PLAY

Foul play is prohibited. Players must not wilfully:

(a) Hack, trip, or strike an opponent.

(b) Hold a player not in possession of the ball.

(c) Cause a scrum to collapse.

Misconduct is prohibited.

For any of these offences the referee will award a penalty kick at the place of infringement. He will caution the player, and he *may* order the player off the field. In the event of that player repeating the offence, the referee *will* order him off the field.

SEVENS

Played on the same sized playing area as the normal game, seven men only are used, and the game lasts seven minutes each way with one minute half time. It is very difficult to play sevens flat out and the winning team will be the one which can control the tempo and tire the opposition by clever tactics.

The ideal team will contain intelligent and intuitive players who are able to work hard and keep possession, positional play is vital and the team should be spread out in order to provide immediate cover whenever required, players not in possession must run in position to support the man with the ball.

An exciting game to play and watch, there is little time for recovery after a successful attack. It's all action!

RUGBY FOOTBALL UNION PUBLICATIONS
(*Available from the Rugby Football Union, Twickenham*)

PUBLICATIONS
Available from Secretary, Rugby Football Union, Twickenham

"**Rugby Football Union Handbook**" including Bye-Laws, Laws of the Game, Affiliated Clubs and Secretaries' addresses. Names and addresses of R.F.U. Committee and Secretaries of National Unions. Fixtures, etc. **Price 50p** per copy.

"**Laws of the Game with Instructions to Referees and Notes for Guidance of Players**". **Price 10p** per copy.

"**Why the Whistle Went**". A popular illustrated book, giving simple and helpful explanation of the Laws of the Game. Revised September 1970. **Price 15p** per copy.
County Unions. Referees Societies, Clubs and Schools may purchase parcels of 20 or more at the special price of **10p** per copy.

"**Rugger—How to Play the Game**". The booklet is illustrated and the text makes amusing and instructive reading. **Price 15p** per copy.
County Unions, Referee Societies, Clubs and Schools may purchase parcels of 20 or more at the special price of **10p** per copy.

"**A Guide for Coaches**". A series of 10 Coaching Pamphlets, inserted in a special R.F.U. loose-leaf Binder. **Price £3** per copy.

"**A Guide for Players**". This publication, which replaces "Basic Skills" is a 70-page booklet, up to date, and well illustrated. It is the players' equivalent to the "Guide for Coaches". **Price 37p** per copy.
County Unions, Referees Societies, Clubs and Schools may purchase parcels of 20 or more at the special price of **33p** per copy.

"**The Art of Refereeing**". **Price 15p** per copy.

"**Training for Rugby Football**". This publication has sections on Basic Training (which could be helpful to anyone), Toughening Training, Combined Training in the Field, Circuit Training and Weight Training. All exercises are well illustrated. **Price 15p** per copy.

"**Rugby Football Schools Union Handbook, 1971-72**". **Price 10p** per copy.

Wall Charts (produced by W.R.U.) Set of 8—Handling, Ruck/Maul, etc. **£1·15** per set.

"**Touchdown**" **Price 45p** per copy.
For multiples of 10 copies—**35p** each.
(*Prices include packaging and postage within United Kingdom only*)

"**INSTANT RUGBY**"
This is an eight-page pocket-sized illustrated leaflet with the sub-title "a 5 minute Guide to the Laws most players have trouble with".

	Direct Purchase (over the counter at Twickenham)	By post (paid) within U.K.	By post (paid) outside U.K.
Single copy ..	3p	5p	10p
Packets of 20 ..	50p	55p	75p
Cartons of 50 (with display poster)..	100p	£1·15	£1·50

FILM SERVICE
A. HIRE SERVICE to member Clubs and Schools in England only
The films in the following list will be subject to a **£1·50 hire charge** to cover administration costs.
"*A New Look at Rugby*". South African Jubilee Matches in 1964 (20 mins.).
"*The Laws of Rugby Union Football*". Explanation of Laws in context of the game (27 mins.).
"*All Blacks Tour 1967—Highlights*". Excerpts from games against England, Scotland and Barbarians (40 mins.).
"*Highlights International Championships 1968-69*". (50 mins.).
"*Highlights International Championships 1969-70*". (40 mins.).
"*Highlights International Championships 1970-71*". (45 mins.).
"*Highlights International Championships 1971-72*". (45 mins.).
"*A Pride of Lions*"—New Zealand Tour 1971 (45 mins.).
"*Barbarians v. South Africa, January, 1970*". High scoring match (40 mins.).
"*France v. England, April, 1970*". High scoring match (40 mins.).
"*France v. England*". Score 37-12. February 1972. (40 mins.).
All the above films are sound, 16 mm. A "silent" film can be projected on a machine built for sound, BUT sound films **MUST NOT** be used on a silent machine. Booking forms for the above films obtainable from Rugby Football Union, Twickenham. <u>Four weeks' notice is required.</u>

C. SALES SERVICE
Films available for Purchase on request.
"*Highlights International Championships 1970-71*".
"*Highlights International Championships 1971-72*".
"*A Pride of Lions*"—New Zealand Tour 1971.
Warwickshire v. Gloucestershire. C.C. Final 1972. } approx. 40-45 mins.
France v. England 1972.
Scotland v. England 1972.
Wales v. France 1972.
All the above films are 16 mm. sound Black and White and orders are to be sent to: The Secretary, Rugby Football Union, Twickenham, Middlesex.
"*A New Look at Rugby*". Extracts from games played in South Africa in 1964 Jubilee Season (20 mins.). Price **£19·00**.
"*Freedom to Run*". A coaching film concentrating on attack—1967 (25 mins.). Price **£25·00**.
Both films black and white, 16 mm. sound. Enquiries and orders for these two films should be sent to: Promotions Department, Associated Newspapers Ltd., Carmelite House, London, E.C.4.
Seeing Sport Series
Four 16 mm. sound films each of 22 minutes' duration. Price **£24·20** each part.
Part 1. *Pre-season Training*. Part 3. *Kicking*.
Part 2. *Passing*. Part 4. *Tackling*.
Enquiries and orders for these four films to be sent to: Town and Country Productions Ltd., 21 Cheyne Row, Chelsea, London, S.W.3.
Note: All prices quoted are liable to amendment without notice.

INDEX

Printed in Great Britain by John Blackburn Ltd., Leeds 10